NAVAJO GIRL

Copyright © 2022 Maureen's Clans

No part of this book may be reproduced or transmitted in any form or by any means, electronic or mechanical, including photocopying, recording or by any information storage and retrieval system, without written permission from the author, except for the inclusion of brief quotations in a review.

Disclaimer:

This book is designed to provide information and motivation to our readers. It is sold with the understanding that the publisher is not engaged to render any type of psychological, legal, or any other kind of professional advice. The content of each article is the sole expression and opinion of its author, and not necessarily that of the publisher. No warranties or guarantees are expressed or implied by the publisher's choice to include any of the content in this volume. Neither the publisher nor the individual author(s) shall be liable for any physical, psychological, emotional, financial, or commercial damages, including, but not limited to, special, incidental, consequential or other damages. Our views and rights are the same: You are responsible for your own choices, actions, and results.

Permission should be addressed in writing to ms.utahglobe2013@icloud.com

Editor: Alison Burney

Book Layout: Amit Dey (amit@hasmarkpublishing.com)

Illustrator: Matrix Media Solutions (vivek@matrixnmedia.com)

ISBN 13: 978-1-77482-071-1
ISBN 10: 1774820714

Dedication

Yá'át'ééh, this book is dedicated to my grandchildren Wolf, Willow and my future grandchildren to come. To my husband Heriberto my love. Our children Justine, Preston, Jaylynn, Yennika and Yadiel. To my siblings Melissa, Madeline and Darel. My nieces and nephews, Hannah, Brave, Navani, Eddie, Mia, Ava, Tea', Addie, and Brennen. To my mom and dad. To all the children everywhere that grow up to celebrate their stories and dreams. Hózhó náhásdlíí'.

This bluebird in Navajo is Dólii (Doe-lee).
We can share them.

This butterfly in Navajo is K'aalógii (Ka-low-gee).
We can share them.

This rabbit in Navajo is Gah (Gau).
We can share them.

This cat in Navajo is Mósí (Mow-see).
We can share them.

This wolf in Navajo is Mą'iitsoh (Ma-eat-so).
We can share them.

This corn in Navajo is Naadą́ą́ (Nah-dah).
We can share them.

This elk in Navajo is Dzééh (Zzeh).
We can share them.

This sheep in Navajo is Dibé (Di-be).
We can share them.

This chipmunk in Navajo is Hazéíts'ósíí (Hay-zays-o-see).
We can share them.

This land is Kéyah (Key-yah) is Navajo.
We can share her too

About the Author

Maureen's paternal grandfather's clan is Water's Edge, her father's clan is Sleepy Rock, and her mother's is Bilagáana (English/Irish).

Maureen has a love for beauty in all things, which, in Navajo, means Hózhó. Maureen graduated pre-med with a Bachelor of Science in Anthropology from the University of Utah, which brings her love of culture, beauty, and science together. She is a business owner of Turquoise, which focuses on beauty in mind with attention to skincare, fitness, beauty, and wellness in a breakdown of behavioral changes over time for her clients. She is an accomplished concert pianist and has been writing her own sonatas since age five. She plays both musicality and prima vista.

Maureen is a national beauty queen, winning more than five state titles and three national ones including Mrs. Utah America, where she was featured by the Navajo Times as the first Dine' (meaning Navajo) to win that title. She also went on to win the title as Mrs. Native America Globe, becoming the first to hold that title as well in Shenzhen, China, with Mrs. North America Classique Globe following years later. Her current title, Mrs. Puerto Rico World, has been featured on the news and in local papers and magazines along with the others.

Maureen's greatest joy and accomplishment is her family: her husband, Heriberto Rivera, from Puerto Rico; their children, Justine, Preston, Jaylynn Yennika and Yadiel; and two cats, Oliver and Ophelia. She loves her nieces and nephews, brothers and sisters and spends time with them often. Maureen is also a grandmother and wrote this book with her grandchildren, Wolf and Willow, as well as her family in mind. She wanted to leave a piece of her culture with them—and now all of you. She hopes you enjoy it.

With every donation, a voice will be given to the creativity that lies within the hearts of our children living with diverse challenges.

By making this difference, children that may not have been given the opportunity to have their Heart Heard will have the freedom to create beautiful works of art and musical creations.

Donate by visiting
HeartstobeHeard.com

We thank you.

www.ingramcontent.com/pod-product-compliance
Lightning Source LLC
Chambersburg PA
CBRC091452160426
43209CB00023B/1873